A BOOK OF SONGS: MY JOURNEY FROM WORRY TO WORSHIP

Prayers and Meditations From My Heart

Erica Averett

A Worshipping Woman Publication

Disclaimer:
The ideas and experiences contained in this book belong solely to the author and are purposed to uplift, encourage, and inspire. This information is not to be used in place of proper medical advice from a qualified medical professional.
If you have feelings of suicide please call someone.
1-1-1: The Father, The Son, The Holy Ghost
9-1-1: Emergency
800-273-8255: National Suicide Prevention Lifeline
DON'T EVER GIVE UP!

Dedicated to Our Father in Heaven.

"All that I am is because of all that You Are."

Revelation 1:8
*I AM ALPHA AND OMEGA, THE BEGINNING AND THE
ENDING, saith the Lord, WHICH IS, AND WHICH WAS,
AND WHICH IS TO COME, THE ALMIGHTY.*

CONTENTS

INTRODUCTION

Let me start by saying this: I have attempted suicide before. I've been in situations that could have taken my life. But I'm still here. I've been broke, hungry, and homeless. Lived in homes infested with roaches and bedbugs. Married and divorced; twice. Had cars repossessed. Been evicted, even been to jail a couple of times. But I'm still here. I've played the name that baby daddy game, even had a child to die. Had others on their deathbed. But, I am still here. I should be dead or out of my mind.

But GOD!!

Does that mean I don't still struggle? No, I struggle every day. Some days it's a struggle just to get out of bed. Some days I don't make it out, but I know that I am still alright and that God gives me another day to get it right. He has brought my family and me out of situations doctors couldn't even explain. I know he has a plan for my life, and I'm so grateful.

This book is a small compilation of a few of my real prayers that became songs. My personal journey from worry to worship. I'm stepping out of fear and into faith. I know wherever I land, God is with me all the way.

**God is, still, and always will be good. I
am what I am because He is!**

FOREWORD

Psalm 46:10

[10]BE STILL, AND KNOW THAT I AM GOD: I WILL BE EXALTED AMONG THE HEATHEN, I WILL BE EXALTED IN THE EARTH.

Psalm 91:14-16

[14]BECAUSE HE HATH SET HIS LOVE UPON ME, THEREFORE WILL I DELIVER HIM: I WILL SET HIM ON HIGH, BECAUSE HE HATH KNOWN MY NAME. [15]HE SHALL CALL UPON ME, AND I WILL ANSWER HIM: I WILL BE WITH HIM IN TROUBLE; I WILL DELIVER HIM, AND HOUNOUR HIM. [16]WITH LONG LIFE WILL I SATISFY HIM, AND SHEW HIM MY SALVATION.

Psalm 96:1-4

[1]Oh sing unto the Lord a new song: sing
unto the Lord, all the earth.
[2]Sing unto the Lord, bless his name; shew
forth his salvation from day to day.
[3]Declare his glory among the heathen, his wonders
among all people.
[4]For the Lord is great, and greatly to be praised:
he is to be feared above all gods.

POSITIVE AFFIRMATIONS

I am able. I am not afraid. I am BLESSED. I am bold. I am confident. I am courageous. I am enough. I am fearless but fearfully made. I am kind. I am patient. I am lovable. I am loved. I am smart. I am strong. I am the lender and not the borrower. I am the head and not the tail. I am above and not below. I am worth it. I am worthy. I am all things through Christ Jesus. I can do all things through Christ Jesus, and I have the power to tread upon serpents and scorpions and all the power of the enemy because no weapon formed against me shall prosper.

MY STORY

Hello. My name is Erica: and I suffer from
fear. It *was* controlling my life.

I did things I wasn't proud of. I settled for certain things and behaviors because I didn't feel I was worth better. I was scared of looking like I didn't have it all together, scared of being alone, scared of losing people that weren't worth my time in the first place. It caused me so much worry, anxiety, and other problems. I would get so worked up about "NOTHING" because that's exactly what it was, "NOTHING!".

When I used to see the memes and posts on social media with the acronym "F.E.A.R. = False Evidence Appearing Real," I knew what it read but, I never knew what it meant, because in those moments the fear made everything seem so real and caused and irrational way of thinking. I would just be confused, stuck, and going in circles at the same time. Going nowhere, real fast.

This book is not so much about the fear but my journey to overcoming it.

As you begin reading, you may start to wonder why there are different formats in this book: such a paragraph, outline, and bullets. First of all, because I wanted it like that (SMILE!). But for real, I am a visual learner, and I like to read: but honestly, words, just laying on a page sometimes tires me and my eyes. Sometimes, I end up just gazing at the words and have to go back and find my place. Then, I usually end up reading the same page two or three times. Also, I've been told I always seem to do things "backward" or the "hard way." I mean, I do try to do things the "normal" way: but I realized I'm not normal, and I have accepted that (SMILE!). So, this was easier for me to produce and understand. Hopefully, it's easier for you as well.

◆ ◆ ◆

With that being said, here are some of the things I experienced:

I. WORRY & ANXIETY (Over-thinking)

A. I could never just be happy in the moment. Always scared of something bad happening or something going wrong. Thinking things like:

- "what if?"
- "how am I going to do this or pay that?" or "if I do this, then this could happen."
- "when?" "why?" "where?" and "HOW?"
- "did I say the right thing during a conversation earlier in the day or even a week before?
- "am I good enough?" "what's wrong with me?" "am I weird?"
- "who won the argument?"
- I can name so many more, but we don't have time for that (SMILE!)".

B. I never felt like I got enough rest and was weary all the time. Even when I was supposed to be asleep, those things were still going through my mind.

C. Always feeling outcast (although being an outcast isn't that bad, *SMILE!). Basically, just not knowing who I was or what I wanted.

II. PROCRASTINATION

A. I was over-thinking the situations so much until the fear of the outcomes had me paralyzed and unable to make decisions.

B. The decisions I did make weren't really mine. I made them based on what I thought others wanted me to do. Or they were just bad decisions based on what type of instant gratification I could get.

C. I wasn't consistent. I started a lot of things I haven't finished. I would just get weary in the middle of whatever.

D. A lot of things didn't get done.

III. MONEY ISSUES

A. I would be so weary or sick from the anxiety, I couldn't make it to work and wouldn't stay on jobs.

B. Procrastinating led bills to be paid late or not at all, causing late fees, reconnection fees, and credit issues: just bad or no budgeting period.

C. And let's face it, money does affect a lot of things (that's a whole different book. I just had a bit of anxiety thinking about it. *exhales loudly. Whew. Let's move on. Thank You, Jesus!*SMILE!!!)

IV. GUILT & SHAME

A. I would often get caught up thinking and wondering how have the negative things in my life affected other people?

B. Did I do the best I could as a mother, daughter, friend, wife?

C. Has my trauma and baggage affected my kids?

V. DEPRESSION & SOCIAL ISSUES

D. ALL OF THE ABOVE.

Yes, I skipped over A, B, and C; and went straight to the "D." That's another book as well, maybe two. (SMILE!!). I just wanted to see if you were paying attention. But really, all of the things above were intertwined, and throw in all of life's trials during my forty-five years of living. It was a lot. It led to depression, and I became a bit more antisocial. Even though I've never really been into social gatherings: I am the person; that when invited to an event, my first question is, "Who all gone be there?"; and if it's too many people, I'm probably not going. I just don't care for crowds; I will say it has kept me from some events that I actually would have gone to due to just being weary in my mind. I mean, sometimes, it was too much for me to have to think about what to wear or what to even do to my hair. And the excitement of it would soon fizzle out, and I would eventually decide just to stay home.

◆ ◆ ◆

This is not an exhaustive list of the things I went through, but a general rundown. If you are experiencing some of these things, please talk to someone. Don't ever give up!

National Suicide Prevention Lifeline: 800-273-8255

WORSHIP OVER WORRY

Needless to say, this book is not so much about those things but how I'm overcoming those things.

I choose to believe. "I had fainted, unless I believed to see the goodness of the Lord in the land of the living." (PSALM 27:13). I suggest reading all of PSALM 27. I'm going to leave you with ISAIAH 40:30-31 as well.

With that being said, it wasn't as easy as it sounds. I started doing and chasing after things I THOUGH I wanted. Just staying busy so I didn't have to think about those things that bothered me. I still wasn't happy, just busy and tired. I was making myself weary, going in circles, just to end up right back at the starting point. I had already made so many mistakes and was scared of making more mistakes and creating a bigger mess. So once again, I found myself stuck.

BUT, I got tired of being tired. I realized that *I* needed to change. Then, I realized I couldn't do that on my own, not in my strength. So, I, literally, started crying out to God, calling on the name of Jesus; praying and letting Him know my feelings, how lost and confused I felt, praying and asking Him, "Lord, what do You want me to do?,(which is the name of one of the songs) because apparently what *I* was doing was not working (LAUGH!!).

I just really started replacing idle time with things of sustenance. Instead of just watching television, and I can watch some TV (SMILE!), I started learning and doing the things that I like, things that bring me peace;

◆ Writing

◆ Reading

◆ Creating in general

◆ Putting together jigsaw puzzles, well really any type of puzzles; crossword, word search, sudoku, Rubix cube

◆ Learning entrepreneurial skills

◆ Listening to music and making play-lists. I love music. (I think it can change so much)

◆ Taking video piano lessons

◆ CUT OUT THINGS THAT DRAIN MY ENERGY!

◆ CUT OUT THINGS THAT DO NOT BRING ME JOY AND PEACE! INCLUDING NEGATIVE PEOPLE!

I also started to write out my prayers and to read and study the bible more. I'm not going to say I understand a lot of it, but I still choose to study and meditate. I started praying for wisdom and understanding. Trust me, it helps! Even when it seemed like it wasn't, it really was. Sometimes, that would cause an inconsistency because I was looking for immediate results. It was like being on a diet when we don't see the results we think we should: we begin to slack on working out, if we do at all. So it was a constant battle, but I knew I couldn't give up. Then, I started praying for things like consistency, discipline, strength, and peace. I also had to choose to be thankful for what I did see, what I did have, and where I was on my journey. Even though I wasn't where I wanted to be, I wasn't where I used to be. I started to praise God for what He was and is. And I started praising Him in advance for the things I know are coming. It seemed like it was going to be a long time. I started to feel weary again.

BUT then, I started to notice the small things. Little changes in the way I felt, in my attitude, and my life period. The small things do matter!

Looking back at my list of activities, it seems like I like to do a lot of alone activities (SMILE!). I don't know if that's good or bad, but I'm learning things about myself as I write this book. I have learned that I do love my peace, just being at home alone in my secret place, but I do have to live in the world.

So with that being said, it's easy to be at peace and pray when you're home alone; and things are going well. But, I had to learn how to apply it in those every day, out in the world situations because, honestly, it's people in the world that make you want to choke them. It might be your boss, kids, or significant other; I don't know, I'm just saying (LAUGH!); it was hard to think of a bible verse to meditate on in the middle of an argument, especially when most times, I was busy try to prove I was right.

Music helps me through these situations. There were times when I would just feel so much anxiety and so much emotion, but I couldn't pinpoint why I was feeling like that. I didn't have the words to pray because I didn't even know what was wrong at the time, so I would just start singing songs or just humming; and the prayers would come, along with a flood of tears, and I would start feeling peace. I started noticing how my attitude would change for the better afterward. Again, the small things do matter.

I started writing those prayers down along with the ones I was already writing because they often repeated; but, maybe the words were in a different sequence or a different melody depending on my mood. Since I like writing and was working on my relationship with God, the prayers, the writing, and the music just seemed to mesh together. So, I continued to pray, hum, and write.

As I started to study those prayers and bible verses that coincided with them, the songs in this book came about. The idea for the book came later. I studied bible passages, sermons on YouTube, and other books and reference materials; I told you I was all over the place (SMILE!), so, at first, there was no consistency in those things. But most of all, I just started depending on God more and letting Him fight my battles. Everything does not need a response. I spend more time praying, asking, and just being thankful, especially for the little things. Now, I have more joy and peace, and I continue to learn things about myself every day; and as a result of this process, I'm developing more consistency and confidence.

As I said earlier, I have started a lot of things and projects that I never finished. So, this will actually be my first finished project (PRAISE BREAK!) THANK YOU, JESUS! It is special and close to my heart. I struggled to push this book out, and even though I'm not finished yet, I continue to pray and have faith that by me gaining the confidence to share my story, it will inspire someone to develop or strengthen their relationship with God and push through their fears. God is waiting for you.

◆ ◆ ◆

While some of the songs seem like they are not complete because they are so short, but they are. Remember the little things matter. I usually hum or sing the stanza and go where ever the Spirit leads me. I don't know where this journey is taking me, **BUT I'm here for it!**
Stay tuned!

To anyone reading this book that I may have offended,
ever, in life, I am truly sorry. No harm intended.

Pray With Me!

Dear Father God, I come to You now, in the humblest way I know how, praying that You keep us wrapped in Your arms. Keep our minds and bodies and that of our loved ones safe from the enemy. Help us please, O Lord, to focus, not on the things going on around us, but on You alone. Keep our thoughts and paths directed toward You, Lord. We are sorry for the times when we stray away. Lord, we are sorry. Please forgive us, Father God. Thank You for coming back to rescue us with open arms. Please help us let go of anything that we are holding on to that keeps our arms from reaching out to you. Thank You that we are above and not below. Thank You for the awesome Father that You are. In Jesus' name, we pray. Amen, Amen, and Amen.

LOVE, PEACE, AND BLESSINGS

A BOOK OF SONGS:

My Journey From Worry To Worship

◆ ◆ ◆

Prayers & Meditations From My Heart

Psalm 100

[1]Make a joyful noise unto the Lord, all ye lands. [2]Serve the Lord with gladness: come before his presence with singing. [3]Know ye that the Lord he is God: it is he that hath made us, and not we ourselves; we are his people, and the sheep of his pasture. [4]Enter into his gates with thanksgiving, and into his courts with praise: be thankful unto him, and bless his name. [5]For the Lord is good; his mercy is everlasting; and his truth endureth to all generations.

Psalm 19:14

[14]Let the words of my mouth, and the meditation of my heart, be acceptable in thy sight, O Lord, my strength, and my redeemer.

Psalm 34:1-3

[1]I will bless the Lord at all times: his praise shall continually be in my mouth. [2]My soul shall make her boast in the Lord: the humble shall hear thereof, and be glad. [3]O magnify the Lord with me, and let us exalt his name together.

◆ ◆ ◆

BELIEVE

He said He'd be there for me.
He said He'd give me what I need.
All I have to do,
Is just believe.

He has a plan for me.
To fulfill my destiny.
He said I love you just because you're you.
Lord, I just want to give You glory.

Matthew 6:33
BUT SEEK YE FIRST THE KINGDOM OF GOD,
AND HIS RIGHTEOUSNESS; AND ALL THESE
THINGS SHALL BE ADDED UNTO YOU.

Psalm 27:13
I had fainted, unless I had believed to see the goodness
of the Lord in the land of the living.

Jeremiah 29:11-13
[11]FOR I KNOW THE THOUGHTS THAT I THINK TOWARD YOU,
saith the Lord, THOUGHTS OF PEACE, AND NOT OF EVIL, TO
GIVE YOU AN EXPECTED END. [12]THEN SHALL YE CALL UPON
ME, AND YE SHALL GO AND PRAY UNTO ME, AND I WILL
HEARKEN UNTO YOU. [13]AND YE SHALL SEEK ME, AND FIND ME,
WHEN YE SHALL SEARCH FOR ME WITH ALL YOUR HEART.

DEAR LORD

Dear Lord, I pray.
Please keep my mind straight.
Don't let me go astray.

Dear Lord, I pray.
These tears I cry, don't let me cry another day.
Please make them go away.

Dear Lord, I pray.
Thank you for making sure I'm safe.
Thank you for making a way.

2 Thessalonians 3:3
But the Lord is faithful, who shall stablish
you, and keep you from evil.

Psalm 59:9
Because his strength will I wait upon thee: for God is my defence.

Psalm 121:7-8
[7]The Lord shall preserve thee from all evil: he shall preserve
thy soul. [8]The Lord shall preserve thy going out and thy
coming in from this time forth, and even for evermore.

BROK-EN

I'm brok-en.
Lord, I need you now.
Lord, I'm brok-en
You say let you in. Please show me how.
Lord, I'm brok-en.
I give You my heart so You can mend.
Lord, I'm brok-en.
Put me back together again.

I'm brok-en.
Lord, I stretch my hands out to You.
Lord, I'm brok-en.
Please, make me new.
Lord, I'm brok-en.
You say things are not as they seem.
Lord, I'm brok-en.
I give You my heart. Please make it clean.

Psalm 38:8
I am feeble and sore broken: I have roared by
reason of the disquietness of my heart.

Psalm 51:7-10
[7]Purge me with hyssop, and I shall be clean: wash me, and I
shall be whiter than snow. [8]Make me to hear joy and gladness;
that the bones which thou hast broken may rejoice. [9]Hide thy
face from my sins, and blot out all mine iniquities. [10]Create in
me a clean heart, O God; and renew a right spirit within me.

Joel 2:12
THEREFORE ALSO NOW, saith the Lord, TURN YE
EVEN TO ME WITH ALL YOUR HEART, AND WITH FASTING,
AND WITH WEEPING, AND WITH MOURNING:

WHAT DO YOU WANT ME TO DO?

What do You want me to do?
I'm here for You.
What do You want me to do?
I'm so confused.
What do You want me to do?
I put my trust in You.
What do You want me to do?
I'm here for You to use.

In the middle of the night, I'm calling on You. I just need
You to hold me tight. In my ear, you whisper, the battle's
not yours to fight. Everything dark will come to light. Just
keep on believing and seeking. In me, please delight.

CHORUS

In the middle of the day, I'm calling on You. I just need
You to slide my way. Then You pull me near and whisper
in my ear. Just keep on believing and speaking. Delight
yourself in me. And I will give you what you need.

CHORUS

All-day long, I'm thanking You for all the things You do, how
You brought me through. So I am here for You to use.

CHORUS

Proverbs 2:3
Yea, if thou criest after knowledge, and liftest
up thy voice for understanding;

Psalm 90:17
And let the beauty of the Lord God be upon us: and
establish thou the work of our hands upon us; yea,
the work of our hands establish thou it.

Psalm 56:4

In God I will praise his word, in God I have put my trust; I will not fear what flesh can do unto me.

LET IT GO

Let it go.
Don't let it hold you down no more.
Let it go.
Don't return to it no more.

All of the pain
And excess baggage;
Give it to God.
For you, He'll carry.

He said Come to me, you heavy laden.
Give me your burdens.
I will carry.
Give it to God.

I give it to You.
I give You the hurt and pain I carry.
I give it to you, Lord.
You can have it.

Matthew 11:28-30
[28]COME UNTO ME, ALL YE THAT LABOUR AND ARE HEAVY
LADEN, AND I WILL GIVE YOU REST. [29]TAKE MY YOKE
UPON YOU, AND LEARN OF ME; FOR I AM MEEK AND
LOWLY IN HEART: AND YE SHALL FIND REST UNTO YOUR
SOULS. [30]FOR MY YOKE IS EASY, AND MY BURDEN IS LIGHT.

Psalm 38:4
For mine iniquities are gone over mine head: as an
heavy burden they are too heavy for me.

Psalm 34:14
Depart from evil, and do good; seek peace, and pursue it.

STRENGTHEN ME

Lord, strengthen my mind.
So I can think like You.
Lord, strengthen my mind.
So I can do like You.

Lord, strengthen my hands.
Cause I got work to do.
Lord, strengthen my hands.
So I can do what You need me to.

Lord, strengthen my body.
So I can go where You need me to go.
Lord, strengthen my body.
So I can move when You say so.

Lord, strengthen my voice.
So I can speak like You.
Lord, strengthen my voice.
So I can say it how You need me to.

Lord, strengthen my heart.
So I can love like You.
Lord, strengthen my heart.
So I can love who You say to.

Lord, strengthen my eyes.
So I can see like You.
Lord, strengthen my eyes.
So I can enjoy this beautiful view.

Strengthen me. Strengthen me.
I got work to do, things to see.
Ooh, strengthen me.
I got people to love and places to be.
Ooh, strengthen me.

Nehemiah 6:9

For they all made us afraid, saying, Their hands shall be weakened from the work, that it be not done. Now therefore, O God, strengthen my hands.

Psalm 138:3
In the day when I cried thou answeredst me, and strengthenedst me with strength in my soul.

2 Corinthians 12:9
And he said unto me, MY GRACE IS SUFFICIENT FOR THEE: FOR MY STRENGTH IS MADE PERFECT IN WEAKNESS.

Philippians 4:13
I can do all things through Christ which strengtheneth me.

I'LL PRAISE YOU

Lord, I don't know what I'd do without You.
So I praise You.
So I praise You.
Lord, I don't know what I'd do, so I'll stick to You like glue.
And I'll praise You.
And I'll praise You.
Lord, I don't know what I'd do, but I know You stay so true.
That's why I praise You.
That's why I praise You.
You pick me up when I am blue.
Cleaned me up and made me new.
So I'll praise You.
So I'll praise You.

Isaiah 25:1
O Lord, thou art my God; I will exalt thee, I will praise
thy name; for thou hast done wonderful things; thy
counsels of old are faithfulness and truth.

Psalm 138:1-2
[1]I will praise thee with my whole heart: before the gods will I
sing praise unto thee. [2]I will worship toward thy holy temple,
and praise thy name for thy lovingkindness and for thy truth:
for thou hast magnified thy word about all thy name.

Psalm 145:1-3
[1]I will extol thee, my God, O king; and I will bless thy name
for ever and ever. [2]Every day will I bless thee; and I will
praise thy name for ever and ever. [3]Great is the Lord, and
greatly to be praised; and his greatness is unsearchable.

LEAD ME

Lead me, guide me, hold my hand.
Lead me, guide me, help me stand.
Lead me, guide me. You have a plan.
Lead me, guide me. You are the man.

Lead me, guide me, hold my hand.
Lead me, guide me, all through the land.
Lead me, guide me, as only You can.
Lead me, guide me. You are the man.

Psalm 143:10
Teach me to do thy will; for thou art my God: thy spirit
is good; lead me into the land of uprightness.

Isaiah 48:17
Thus saith the Lord, thy Redeemer, the Holy One of
Israel; I AM THE LORD THY GOD WHICH TEACHETH
THEE TO PROFIT, WHICH LEADETH THEE BY
THE WAY THAT THOU SHOULDEST GO.

Psalm 16:11
Thou wilt shew me the path of life: in thy presence is fulness
of joy; at thy right hand there are pleasures for evermore.

HOLD ME

I need You to hold me, in the palm of Your hand.
I need You to rock me, like only You can.
I need You to hold me, like You said You would.
I need You to rock me. I know Your word is good.

I need You to rock me, all during the night.
I need You to hold me in the morning light.
I need You to rock me through the midst of my storm.
I need You to hold me, as I yet mourn.

Psalm 139:8-10

[8]If I ascend up into heaven, thou art there: if I make my bed in hell, behold, thou art there. [9]If I take the wings of the morning, and dwell in the uttermost parts of the sea; [10]Even there shall thy hand lead me, and thy right hand shall hold me.

2 Corinthians 1:3-4

[3]Blessed be God, even the Father of our Lord Jesus Christ, the Father of mercies, and the God of all comfort; [4]Who comforteth us in all our tribulations, that we may be able to comfort them which are in any trouble, by the comfort wherewith we ourselves are comforted of God.

Psalm 77:6

I call to remembrance my song in the night: I commune with mine own heart: and my spirit made diligent search.

THANK YOU

Have I told You thank You today?
For keeping me safe. Always. 24/7. No delays.
You're always on time. You're always on time.

I just wanna tell You thank You always.
For making a way. Everyday. 24 hours. Let me count the ways.
You're always on time. You're always on time.

1 Chronicles 16:34
O give thanks unto the Lord; for he is good;
for his mercy endureth for ever.

Psalm 103:1
Bless the Lord, O my soul: and all that is
within me, bless his holy name.

Psalm 104:33-34
[33]I will sing unto the Lord as long as I live: I will sing
praise to my God while I have my being. [34]My meditation
of him shall be sweet: I will be glad in the Lord.

FREE

I'm waiting on You.
You're waiting on me.
To see.
The me, You created me to be; Marvelously.

I'm waiting on You.
You're waiting on me.
To be.
Who You created me to be; Fearless and Free.

John 8:32
AND YE SHALL KNOW THE TRUTH, AND THE
TRUTH SHALL MAKE YOU FREE.

Psalm 139:14
I praise thee; for I am fearfully and wonderfully made; marvellous
are thy works; and that my soul knoweth right well.

Psalm 118:23
This is the Lord's doing; it is marvellous in our eyes.

YOU ARE

All that I am,
Is cause of all that You are.
You are the Precious Lamb.
My Bright and Morning Star.

You are my joy.
You are my peace.
Lord, You are the only thing,
That matters to me.

You are my strength.
The wind beneath my wings.
Lord, You are my everything.
You are my King.

Jesus, You are, You are, You are.
You are the only thing,
That matters to me.
Jesus, You are, You are, You are.
You are my everything.
You are my King.

There's nothing they can do,
To come between me and You.
I'll abide in You,
Your word is true.
Long as I got You,
I can't lose.

Jesus, You are, You are, You are.
You are the only thing,
That matters to me.
Jesus, You are, You are, You are.
You are my everything.
You are my King.

Revelation 1:8

I AM ALPHA AND OMEGA, THE BEGINNING AND THE ENDING, saith the Lord, WHICH IS, AND WHICH WAS, AND WHICH IS TO COME, THE ALMIGHTY.

Psalm 119:160

Thy word is true from the beginning: and every one of thy righteous judgments endureth for ever.

Psalm 95:1-3

[1]O come, let us sing unto the Lord: let us make a joyful noise to the rock of our salvation. [2]Let us come before his presence with thanksgiving, and make a joyful noise unto him with psalms. [3]For the Lord is a great God, and a great King above all gods.

GLORY

I know my happiness comes from You.
So I'll stick to You like glue.
Watch You do what You do.
All of my happiness comes from You.

All the glory belongs to You.
No one can do what You do.
You always come through.
All the glory belongs to You.

All the praise belongs to You.
Your word is always true.
There's nothing that You can't do.
All of my praise belongs to You.

Philippians 4:6-7
[4]Be careful for nothing; but in every thing by prayer and supplication with thanksgiving let your requests be made known unto God. [7]And the peace of God, which passeth all understanding, shall keep your hearts and minds through Christ Jesus.

Psalm 30:11-12
[11]Thou hast turned for me my mourning into dancing: thou hast put off my sackcloth, and girded me with gladness; [12]To the end that my glory may sing praise to thee, and not be silent. O Lord my God, I will give thanks unto thee for ever.

Psalm 149:5
Let the saints be joyful in glory: let them
sing aloud upon their beds.

FIRE

You are the fire to my flame.
Lord, with You, I feel no shame.
You are the fire to my flame.
You gave me sunshine, when all I had was rain.

You are the fire to my flame.
You give me peace in the midst of my pain.
You are the fire to my flame.
You gave me hope, when You took the blame.

Romans 12:11
Not slothful in business; fervent in spirit; serving the Lord;

2 Timothy 1:6-8
[6]Wherefore I put thee in remembrance that thou stir
up the gift of God, which is in thee by the putting on of
my hands. [7]For God hath not given us the spirit of fear;
but of power, and of love, and of a sound mind.

Psalm 107:29
He maketh the storm a calm, so that the waves thereof are still.

FOR EVERMORE

My love is Yours.
For evermore.
Our love will soar.
'Cuz Your love is pure.
It's wonderful.
So incredible.

My love is Yours.
For evermore.
This love will soar.
'Cuz Your love's so pure.
So beautiful.
It's so wondrous.

Psalm 86:10-12
[10]For thou art great, and doest wondrous things: thou art God alone. [11]Teach me thy way, O Lord; I will walk in thy truth: unite my heart to fear thy name. [12]I will praise thee, O Lord my God, with all my heart: and I will glorify thy name for evermore.

Philippians 4:8
Finally, brethren, whatsoever things are true, whatsoever things are honest, whatsoever things are just, whatsoever things are pure, whatsoever things are lovely, whatsoever things are of good report; if there be any virtue, and if there be any praise, think on these things.

Psalm 105:5
Remember his marvellous works that he hath done; his wonders, and the judgments of his mouth;

ABOUT THE AUTHOR
Erica Averett

Lover of God and music, mother, writer; to be continued... God is not finished with her yet. There is no telling where she will end up next on her journey from worry to worship!

www.ingramcontent.com/pod-product-compliance
Lightning Source LLC
Chambersburg PA
CBHW060638030426
42337CB00018B/3397